STANDING LONELY IN THE ALLEY

KEN TOMARO

PRAISE FOR *STANDING LONELY IN THE ALLEY*

Ken Tomaro's new collection of poetry is a bitter tour de force of grief and disappointment, with humor guiding the poems throughout the chapbook. Ken writes with an acerbic wit in conversational free verse. Read him for his expression of life's surprise and often tragic-comic experience and read him for his craft.

Robert Allen, author of *Big Blue Hospital and Other Poems*

Ken Tomaro's no-nonsense approach to poetry is ostensibly influenced by decades of adversity and the stressful ups-and-downs of daily life. However, the brilliance lies in the interwoven humor softening and sometimes mocking the sad and often dark corners of our lives. While this may admittedly be unintentional, the recurring harsh tone and subject matter of Ken's words regularly hint at an underlying layer of optimism. His stark, observational style is undeniable yet he occasionally recalls vignettes from his childhood bringing additional flavors of nostalgia and sentimentality into his poetry. Ken sums up his personal trajectory best:
"I certainly don't have it straight and level now but straighter than it has been".

Tom Heath, fan and friend since 1982

In *Standing Lonely in the Alley,* Ken is a master chef, skilled at combining nostalgia, humor, pointed observations of life, and gut punches into a tasty dish of words you won't forget.

Nolcha Fox, author of *Words into Elephants*, *Cancer Isn't Just a Constellation* and others.

Gnashing Teeth Publishing
242 East Main Street
Norman AR 71960
http://GnashingTeethPublishing.com

Printed in the United States of America

ISBN

Library of Congress Control Number:

Non-Fiction: Poetry

Gnashing Teeth Publishing First Edition

TABLE OF CONTENTS

No. God damn it, I'm sick of it...and page numbers too!

I am but an aphid chewing the leaves of a tomato plant and counting the days

there is a scent in the air
of fresh tomatoes floating in a pot of water
ready to be rinsed, cooked down and
poured into glass jars
mixed with the smell of a musty dank basement
the daddy long legs call home
the cars on the highway are big steel machines
I watch the numbers on the gas pump
roll like a combination lock
as my mother fills the tank
I can see the fumes floating off the nozzle
the lake we would go swimming on a quiet Saturday, is gone
covered over and turned into a hospice care facility
the woods behind the house are gone
to make room for more houses
the photo huts are gone
the movie theaters, dime stores are gone
my childhood is gone
my 20s, 30s, 40s gone
my hair, eyesight
everything has been demolished, buried, and rebuilt
leaving only memories
memories of something as simple as
fresh tomatoes floating in a pot of water

Will we remember when we're gone?

I remember one of the sillier things as a child
that seems so strange now
she would hang plastic eggs
on a tree in the front yard for the Easter holiday
dozens of them
like you or I would decorate a Christmas tree
it just didn't seem like her
but after a while she didn't seem like her

Sharing the wealth

they all have the plague
they all have had it
and act like they can't get it again
spitting in the wind
coughing and sniffling in the clean air
they're all licking doorknobs
and grabbing their crotches
touching his stuff
and her stuff
and my stuff
they've all had the plague
and want to take everyone else down with them
scratching their heads and wondering
why everyone is dead
or on death's door
or in death's bed

Jumping the shark to get to the bandwagon

ah, there it is again
some hot young thing
got ahold of the latest fashion footwear
and everyone else jumps on that train
pretty soon the 40 and 50-year-olds
think they can pull it off
and now everyone is walking around
like they are stepping barefoot on broken glass
some days all you can do
is laugh at this silly little world

A product of the time

those who didn't smoke cigarettes smoked pot
and called everyone else out
those who didn't smoke pot
drank whiskey and beer
and called everyone else out
those who didn't drink whiskey and beer
rolled the dice or bet on the horses
and called everyone else out
and of course, those who didn't drink,
smoke, roll the dice, or bet on the horses
preached their various religions and
called everyone else out

A playing field that is anything but level

if I think back to how it was
I certainly don't have it straight and level now
but straighter than it has been
and that says something

Breaking the cycle (or a broken bicycle)

you know, you have these days
where everything is the same
nothing really good happens
nothing really bad
just more of the same
and you sit waiting for the dam to break
for all those good things
to come flooding out at once
and you wait
and you wait...

Throwing your cares to the wind

she used to write all her problems,
those things she wanted to let go of
on sticks and pieces of driftwood
and throw them in the lake
never thinking they would wash back up on shore
as if her problems didn't want to let go of her

Or so the letters behind my name tell me

they say, "that's why you make the big bucks!"
and I say, to myself,
"no no, I make just enough
to make things harder for all of us.
just enough to fuck things up a little."
I wake up at the ass-crack of dawn
just for you
there was a priest on the TV
telling a gypsy she was a fool
and the gypsy telling the priest the same
and I agreed with both of them
but that's why I make the big bucks

50 cents'll getcha

with age comes wisdom
and the wisdom to know
life isn't so enjoyable the older you get
not like it was when you were a child
and 2 quarters in your pocket meant
you had it all
now you wake up
sometimes angry for no reason
you make grunting noises
as you fall out of bed
you stumble into the bathroom
to pound out a shit that doesn't want to come
you drive the same road to work every day
you sit at a desk in an office at a job
that is killing you
and you are aware of all of this
get another job you say?
it doesn't work like that
you have to know someone who knows someone
you have to network
and talk to people
you have to know how to talk, how to bullshit
to sit at another desk for another job
that will kill you
you might have money to take a vacation
but probably not
and you wouldn't know where to go
even if you could
so you take the 2 quarters out of your pocket
buy a handful of little rubber balls from a machine
and spend your time bouncing them
against the side of the grade school wall
and you think to yourself,
oh shit, I lost one on the roof
but you remember you have a pocketful
and you smile a little

Turkey leg

I've completed another leg
of this thing called life
—another work week over,
my back a little stiffer
but the bills are paid
it's still cold here
Mother Nature, man...
she really likes to keep her bony little fingers
around the jugular
if the world and everyone in it
has to accept every constant change
why can't she let go without a fight?
it is time,
the tulips are sprouting as the snow falls,
they don't care
ah well, I'll cook some fish for dinner
maybe smoke a joint

I sit watching an old movie
something about a bridge
over a river in Thailand

I have the time
time is...
on my side
time is of the essence
time to fry an egg
time is a construct
a ghost from the past

time to wake up
time to forget

to die
water the plants
it's time to chase your tail, your dreams
your fame

time to blow up the bridge

If I were the gills of a fish

the sound of a rotary phone spinning its wheel,
that's really something
and there sure is a lot of adultery
in old black-and-white movies
when strangers fell in love
by simply looking into each other's eyes
these fucking Catholics and their fish fries
choking back shot after beer
pretending it's the Christian thing to do
there is bread and Braunschweiger in the fridge
a roll of toilet paper
it'll be an all right day
save the children
save the elephants and save
the polar bears
save yourself
I'm as old as old is
older than mountains, older than
the big bang that started it all,
it's too late for me
the system is strapped to the gills
we're all gonna die like this, left on hold
and if you roll your eyes
when I tell you I've just eaten a fried Spam sandwich
remember, it's food
and we're all lucky to have it

Welcome to America, suck us!

I am not anti-American, a communist
but this country is complete shit
in so many ways
we may not be under the rule of a single dictator
(but many, as a matter of fact)
who drops bombs whenever he gets an itch
we are not slaves or machines
we are human beings
and we are not allowed to have abortions
because the politician cheating on his wife says so
we are not entitled to food and shelter
you have to work hard, 24 hours a day
says the wealthy businessman
we are not allowed to retire on social security
until we are approaching death's doorstep
until we fill out 5 different forms
and wait 6 months to be rejected
pre-existing condition?
sorry, the doctor can't see you now

Pepperidge Farms

I remember the creek in the park
and the tree with a funny bend in it
we climbed on it often
I remember what the principal's office looked like,
the smell of cigarette smoke choking the air
the fort in the woods
with big hairy spiders and
magazines with naked women on every page
the big green car, the rust, the smell of gasoline
the water running through the pipes
Ghoulardi and the Saturday night movie
—fighting like hell to stay awake
the awful Sunday mornings in church
the cowlick in my hair
I remember...
ah, well, I guess some things
even Pepperidge Farms doesn't remember

I've finally made it

there you have it
...sure, you'd rather be on some sunny patio
enjoying a nice $20 meal
with a fancy beer to wash it down
hey, life ain't fair
that's why you're sitting on your bed
in your small yellow room
eating an underripe pear and staring at the cat
life isn't fair
the cat is gone
the pear has become one with Mother Earth again
and you can call yourself the Poet Laureate
of the Cleveland sewer system

On why I don't like poetry

man, I'm not interested
in the shit that was
I'm interested in the shit that is

Was I a jock or a preppy?

I don't remember the rich
talking about being rich
or the poor talking about being poor
I just remember we talked about
who had money and who didn't
without them telling us
who did or didn't

we were too busy
living the lives we were supposed to be living

not the lives according to money

we were kids
and we didn't care who was who
we were just glad the person next to us cared enough

The easy life

there was a man
on the deck of a long cargo ship
moving toward the mouth of the Cuyahoga
he was sitting comfortably on a folding chair
as if he had done this a hundred times before
a beacon guiding the ship
through the winding river
he waved
I waved back
I wish I had it so easy

Like snapping a rubber band

I raise both arms in the air,
scratch my koala-like head
before I tilt it back to stretch my spine

it does no good

I walk through the halls to the bathroom
notice the wallpaper peeling in spots
notice the asparagus
has finally left my system

I walk through the lobby to the escalator
there is a young, attractive girl
coming up as I am going down
she smiles at me, a big smile
I smile back, closed mouth lifting my cheeks
as if I had just sucked on a lemon

for some reason, perhaps
because I am still half asleep,
I can't stop staring at her
too tired to look away
she smiles again
I smile again
and now we are locked in war
she finally passes
and I think to myself,
what the fuck is wrong with you?

I wonder if she thinks I'm some old creep
when all I am is half asleep

the wind outside is blowing me around
as I try to smoke a cigarette
the air is cold
but not cold enough to wake me fully

the pigeons are sharing breakfast
the sidewalks have soaked up the rain

I stretch again
it does no good

and I need to sleep

The warrior

aren't we all
just trying to find our way home?
aren't we all
just skating through life,
fighting off our demons, our past?
aren't we all
just hiding behind makeup and silly costumes?
navigating the subways
and boardwalks and back alleys
looking for love
looking for a place to belong
a place to call home
while the voice in our heads
gives a play by play
quietly day by day
sometimes you're handcuffed in place
with no way out
and sometimes you find the way
and make it to the sunrise
knowing it was never your fault at all

Little bluebirds

snow is pelting the window
the sound of a million spiders
walking across glass
-like radio static in the back of your head
Life is a book you never want to end
but the book and the body
decay the same
and one by one
they line up at the podium
chirping like starving little birds
begging for scraps of praise
and I just read somewhere
a turtle born sometime in the 1800's
just turned 190 years old
slow and steady, they say, wins the race
but everyone is a little tired of running

Returning home

6:30 am and off to work as usual,
stumbling through it
but this day was not the usual for once
the sky was a light ocean blue
against the pastels of newly budding trees
there was no traffic on the roads
no horns honking
no careless humans darting into the streets
the sun was not blinding
it had been cold for so long
things had been bad for so long
I didn't know what to do
or think
so I smiled for a moment
the tulips had bloomed
the colors of starbursts
and probably as sweet
and just like clockwork
while smoking outside at the office
the bums came
begging
doing their best to ruin this moment
I waved them off with guilty arms
the guilt was fleeting
as my brother once said:
I'm tired of dancing around other people's damage
and I noticed the spiders came back to the windows

It is a man's world and the pigeon's aren't having it

the pigeons were feeling frisky this morning
or at least one of them was
the female was disinterested
but the male persisted
like some muscle-bound gore
flexing his guns at the gym
the female had finally had enough,
flew away and kept flying
leaving the male standing there dumbfounded
looking around in disbelief
it reminded me of youth
but son,
not all women melt over rock hard abs

I want

wandering aimlessly
wandering restlessly,
numb, apathetic through the days
wishing these things
that have become my responsibility
because someone else doesn't want the responsibility
would go away
I want to ignore them like everyone else ignores them
I want to lie in the bed and stare at the ceiling
I want to sit in the park watching the water flow
I want to stare out the window of a coffee shop
watching all those things to be written about
and the days come
that I wish for the bottle
but I'm too lazy and responsible to buy a bottle
(although it is easy)
the rancid taste in the back of my throat
is someone else's bitterness
and now I understand why
why we put so much effort into remembering the past,
the escape of it all when we
blew through the days
in our separate ways
and the inside of our outside little worlds
were taken for granted
and our veins pumped the blood—
still do
sometimes it coagulates, sometimes it clumps up,
breaks off
and you remember the past
as you sit babbling like a drunkard
and you remember the past,
wondering if the blood will still flow
and you remember the past
as you grunt getting out of bed
as your bones make popping sounds

as you grab the handrail walking up the stairs
and the people die and fade away
and the path becomes covered
in grass and weeds, then asphalt, then steel
then the past becomes nothing more
than a series of sunsets

And this is why you don't sell

if you're writing to be discovered
if you're writing for approval
if you're writing
to be wrapped in a godly shroud of applause
if you're writing
because you know it all
or think you know it all
if you're writing for the parties
and the praise and the people
if you're writing because you want your wings,
those glorious angel wings
if you're writing for the money,
oh yes, the money
if you're writing to use words like academia
in everyday conversation
words like askance, penultimate,
empyrean, propinquity
if you're writing for control
for the power
if you're writing to win
if you're writing for the biggest prize
if you're writing for the grades
the titles, the tenure
unless you're writing
to bring darkness to the light
or light to the darkness
then, you aren't writing at all
you are simply a blind dog
sniffing around his own pile of shit

Gossip mags

I heard somewhere
if you want to improve your posture
pretend you're shooting lasers from your nipples
and aim for someone's head
which makes as much sense
as anything I guess
but I also heard Burgess Meredith say
to get through the hard times, the long days
close your eyes and picture a farm
a nice little plot of land

pinch your nose
and bob your head up and down
until you need to breathe
to unclog your sinuses

swish olive oil in your mouth
for no less than five minutes
to loosen the plaque

wrap onions on your feet while you sleep
to get rid of foot odor

pour peroxide in your ears
until it stops bubbling to get rid of a cold

how
did we ever make it?

Like roaches from the woodwork

where do the poets go
when they are done poeting?
do they slink back into a crack in the wall
of some dark coffee shop?
do they hang out in front of the mirror
fixing their slick 50's style hair
adjust their retro shades,
their bowling shirts
their tweed jackets and pipes
whispering the word laureate
over and over again
laureate, laureate...until they are convinced?
where do the poets go
when they are done with the word?
are they gypsies
roaming from one reading to the next?
do they sleep amongst the books
of some grand academic library
or in a comfortable hole in the earth?
do they talk about sports
or the Saturday night movie?
do they eat macaroni and cheese?

T-bone and potatoes

once in a great while
you get that feeling in your gut
as you drive through the intersection
the feeling you are about to be t-boned
for no reason, it's just there
you slow down
look both ways
look in front of you
things have been— going lately
not great but ok enough
and you wait for the other shoe to drop
the hammer to fall
the door to shut
the nail in the coffin
the luck of a penny to fail
and so I stood on the balcony
to drown whatever sorrows were eating me
in another cloud of cigarette smoke
the sun hadn't fully set
and the streetlights kicked on
across the driveway were some flowers
blooming over the neighbor's fence
with the lights just right
and the sun just right
the colors of the trees
and the flowers and the sky
were something out of a museum painting
and some of those days
when nothing is great, only ok
it's not what you're looking at
but how you look at it
look quickly though and take it in
because like life, the sun, the lights
the memories
this moment will fade into darkness
and you'll miss it in a single blink

I tried unlocking the secrets of the universe but broke the key off in the door

there you sit
innocently smoking a joint to relax
to take the edge off
and suddenly you open a door
that has unlocked the secrets of the universe

maybe not all the questions
that have been eating away at you
but a couple you felt important enough

only, you wake up the next morning
and remember none of the answers

      the universe's funny little way
      of saying, maybe
      they weren't as important
      as you thought

or maybe you opened
the wrong door
there are so many
to choose from

and maybe none of them are wrong or right

ACKNOWLEDGEMENTS

I should be better about this. A very small thimbleful of these poems (although I don't remember which ones) have been published on Facebook. Don't worry, there are only about 5 people who pay attention. A few have been read aloud in a weekly poetry group I was in. I'm just a guy sitting on the 37th floor of his office yelling into the clouds.

I would like to thank the Thursday Night Poets, the aforementioned group (you know who you are). They listened to my rantings & frustrations of the writing and submitting process. They also gave me a lot of inspiration to keep writing in a world that is barely listening to us poets. I'd also be a complete idiot if I didn't thank the folks at Gnashing Teeth for publishing this collection. I have so much more.

ABOUT THE AUTHOR

Never, until recently, did he consider writing poetry. Not when he slid from the womb. Not when he felt the first tingle of teen hormones. Not after he got married, divorced, moved to another city, lost a couple jobs, moved back. It just sort of happened. Ken Tomaro, self-proclaimed poet laureate of the Cleveland sewer system, has been writing poetry for a few short years. He's not famous, rich, recognized or read in schools across America. He *has* been published in several literary journals, done a couple podcasts, started the YouTube channel, *Screaming Down the Poetic Highway*, and that's pretty damn impressive.

www.ingramcontent.com/pod-product-compliance
Lightning Source LLC
Chambersburg PA
CBHW061328120626
46546CB00007B/2721